HELP IS ON THE WAY FOR:

Book Reports

Written by Marilyn Berry
Pictures by Bartholomew

CHILDRENS PRESS ™

CHICAGO

Childrens Press
School and Library Edition

Producers: Ron Berry and Joy Wilt Berry
Editor: Orly Kelly
Consultant: Georgiana Burt
Design and Production: Abigail Johnston
Typesetting: Curt Chelin

ISBN 0-516-03231-3
Copyright © 1984 by Marilyn Berry
Institute of Living Skills, Fallbrook, CA
All rights reserved.
Printed in the United States of America.

So your teacher assigned another **book report**!

Hang on! Help is on the way!

If you have a hard time—

- choosing a book,
- reading a book, or
- doing book reports. . .

. . .you are not alone.

Just in case you're wondering...

...why don't we start at the beginning?

Did you know that...?

- Books can take you anywhere in the world.

- Books can show you how to make things.

- Books can make you think and give you ideas.

- Books can entertain you.

- Books can let you escape for a while.

- Books can help you deal with your problems.

Why does your teacher want you to read?

Your teacher knows that the more you read, the better a reader you will become.

Your teacher also knows that reading can make your life easier.

Now that you see what's good about books, it's time to choose a book to read.

When your teacher assigns a book report, be sure to find out two things:

1. The date the assignment is due. (Be sure to write down the date so you won't forget it.)

2. What kind of book you are to read.

There are two kinds of books:

fiction and **nonfiction**

Fiction is something that is **not** true. Here are some different kinds of fiction books:

- fantasy—tales of the imagination
- mystery—tales of intrigue
- science fiction—stories based on future scientific possibilities
- romance—love stories
- historical fiction—history based on un-documented past events.

Nonfiction is something that **is** true. Here are some different kinds of nonfiction books:

- biography—someone's life story written by another person
- autobiography—one's own life story written by oneself
- history—history based on documented past events
- instructional—information on how to make and create
- how-to—how to help yourself and others

Sometimes, choosing a book is no easy task.

But don't worry, there are lots of tricks to help you choose the book that's right for you.

First, you can get some recommendations from:

- your friends

- your teachers

- your librarian

When someone recommends a book, be sure to write down the title and author of the book.

You might even want to keep a list called "Books I Want to Read."

Remember, though, only **you** can tell if a book is right for you.

There are several things to remember in choosing the book that's right for you.

Make sure the book is about something that interests you.

Make sure the book is not too difficult to read.

Try this simple trick to determine if a book is too hard for you:

- Choose a passage from the book.
- Count out 100 words.
- Read the 100 words. If you miss five words or more, the book is probably too difficult for you at this time. Keep it on your list and try it again in a few months.

Make sure you enjoy the book.

You do not have to finish every book you start.
A good rule of thumb is:

• Read two chapters or 25 pages, whichever is the
  longest. If you do not like the book at that
  point, put it aside and try another book.

Once you have found a book that is just right for you, it's time to start reading.

Find a comfortable spot, but not **too** comfortable.

Make sure you have proper lighting so you won't strain your eyes.

Try to find a place with few distractions. You need to be able to concentrate.

Give yourself enough time to get into the mood of the book. You'll get more out of your reading.

When you are reading a book for a book report, make sure you finish reading your book on time.

Use this easy formula to set up your schedule:
- Determine how many days you have before your book report is due.
- Subtract seven days (one week) for working on your report. The remainder is the number of days you have for reading.
- Determine the total number of pages of your book. (Look at the last page.)
- Divide the number of pages by the number of days for reading.

This formula will tell you the number of pages that you will need to read each day.

For example, if your report is due in 27 days:

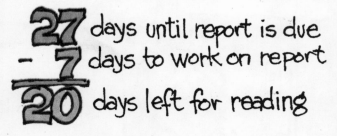

27 days until report is due
− 7 days to work on report
20 days left for reading

If your book has 200 pages:

$$20 \text{ days} \overline{)200 \text{ pages}} = 10 \text{ pages per day}$$

You will need to read at least 10 pages a day. **Try not to fall behind.**

As you are reading, jot down ideas you may want to use for your report.

Write down special thoughts or passages *and* their page numbers. They will come in handy when you put together your report.

When you finish reading your book, it is time to start working on your book report.

This doesn't mean that the fun has to end. Book reports can be fun!

But first, do you know *why* your teacher has you do book reports?

There really *are* some good reasons for doing a book report.

- It lets your teacher know that you have read and understood the whole book.
- It gives you a chance to share your book with others.
- It makes you think about what you have read.
- It helps you organize your thoughts about the book, and learn how to express your opinion.

Before you begin, you will need to decide what kind of book report you want to do. There are many different ways to do book reports. There are **traditional book reports** which follow a simple written format and are especially good for books with story lines. There are also **alternative book reports** which can use—

- artwork,
- drama, or
- creative writing.

Be sure to check with your teacher for approval before you choose any of the following ideas.

The traditional book report is easy to do if you take it one step at a time. There are **four steps** to a traditional book report: the publishing information, the story information, the theme, and your opinion.

Step one—The publishing information is an important part of a book report. It provides the necessary data so that others can locate the book if they decide to read it. You will find most of this information on the first few pages of the book. Make sure you include the following information in your report:

Title: Brent's Invention
Author: John Patterson
Publisher: Star Publishing Co.,
Kansas City, Missouri
Copyright date: 1984
Type of book: Science Fiction

Step two—The story information is a brief description of the book and includes three parts: the setting, the main characters, and the plot.

The setting. To identify the setting of a story, ask yourself two questions: "**Where** does the story take place?" and "**When** does the story take place?" This information may vary with each book. To help you decide which information to include, look for details that are especially important to the story.

The main characters. To identify the main characters in a book, ask yourself, "**Who** is the story about?" This person is usually the main character. Other important characters are also easy to spot. They appear often throughout the book and are important to the overall story. After you identify the main characters, give a brief description of each one.

The plot. To identify the plot of a book, ask yourself, "**What** happens in the story?" The plot will usually include a series of major events that involve the main characters in the book. After you identify these events, give a brief description of each one.

Step three—The theme, or message, of a story deals with the author's purpose for writing the book. To identify the theme of a book, ask yourself, "What is the author trying to say to me?" Sometimes, this may take a little thought on your part. The message of a story is not always plainly stated in the book. But it can be fun to try to discover what point the author is making. Once you identify the theme, describe it and briefly tell how the author got the point across.

Step four—Your opinion is the final part of your book report. It is your chance to discuss how you feel about the book. Regardless of whether you like or dislike a book, it is important for you to explain **why**. If there was a part in the book which you especially enjoyed, this is a good time to mention it briefly.

Alternative book reports. Here are some ideas for alternative book reports that use artwork, drama, and creative writing. These ideas can be used as book reports that stand alone or to supplement traditional book reports. Some of these ideas are especially good for books that do not have story lines.

USING ARTWORK

Collage. Cut pictures from magazines that illustrate something about the book and paste them on poster board.

Poster. Make an advertisement selling the book.

Map. Draw the layout of the city, town, or countryside described in the book.

Book jacket. Make a new jacket for the book, illustrating an exciting scene.

Puzzle. Draw a picture of a scene from the book on poster board, then cut it up in odd-shaped pieces and use as a jigsaw puzzle.

Rebus. Describe a scene in the book using mostly pictures to illustrate the sounds of words, phrases, or syllables.

Chalk talk. Draw pictures on the chalk board as you tell the story to the class.

Mural. Draw several scenes in sequence on large sheets of paper, tape them together and hang on a wall or bulletin board.

Wordless book. Tell the story using only pictures of important scenes from the book.

Portraits. Draw pictures of the characters as you see them in your mind.

Scrapbook. Put together a collection of things that describe the book.

Puppets. Make puppets that resemble the characters in the book.

Sculpture. Make figures of the characters using clay, styrofoam, or other materials.

32

Diorama. Recreate a scene from the book on a table top or in a box, using 3-dimensional figures and a background.

"How-to" creations. Make something that is illustrated in a "how-to" book.

Time line. Illustrate the events in the book, in sequence, along a time line.

Game. Create a board game by drawing connecting squares around the outer edge of a piece of poster board. Illustrate the squares with scenes in the book. The players can be the characters.

USING DRAMA

Some of these ideas are good group projects.

TV advertisement. Perform a TV ad that attempts to sell the book.

Pantomime. Act out a scene without using words.

Talk show. Have a host interview a character in the book, or the ''author.''

Puppet show. Using puppets, act out a scene in the book.

Dramatization. Act out a scene using props.

Radio show. Using only voices and sound effects, act out a scene in the book.

Quiz show. Ask the "contestants" questions that reveal interesting things about the book.

Movie review. Pretend the book has been made into a movie and present a critical review.

Panel of critics. Have a panel discuss the good and bad points of the book.

Music. Put together a musical presentation to accompany the description of the book.

Guest appearance. Pretend you are one of the characters in the book and describe your experiences.

Living picture. Use a large frame and have the characters pose as if in a picture. Have someone describe the scene.

USING WRITING

Here are some different ways to write book reports that are unusual and fun.

Letter to a friend. Describe and recommend the book to your friend.

Letter to the author. Ask the author questions about the book.

Newspaper article. Describe an event in the book as if you were a newspaper reporter and your story was going to appear in your local newspaper.

Crossword puzzle. Make up a puzzle using clues and key words from the book.

Test. Pretend you are a teacher and create a test based on the book.

Script. Write a radio, TV, or movie script based on a scene from the book.

Comparisons. Compare a character with yourself or someone you know.

Gift list. Describe a present you would send to each character in the book and explain your choices.

Poem. Write a poem about the book or one of the characters.

Dear Abby. Write an advice column, answering letters from the characters in the book.

Changes. Write about changes you would have made if you had written the book.

Epilogue. Write about what you think might have happened right after the story ended.

Sequel. Write about what happens twenty years later.

37

Here are some special ideas for book reports that involve a little more time and planning.

- Ask your teacher or librarian about books that have been made into short movies that can be shown to the class.

Introduce the story, show an exciting part of the film (but *not* the ending) so that your friends will want to read the book themselves.

Remember that you will need to plan ahead to reserve the film and to get the equipment necessary to show it.

- Write out questions you would like to ask the author of the book. Send the questions, along with a cassette tape, to the author in care of the publishers. Ask the author to answer the questions on the tape and send it back to you. Be sure to include return postage.

Play the tape for your class.

- Do some research to see if any authors or illustrators live in your area (your librarian can help). Contact one of them and ask if he or she can visit your school for a talk or interview.

Here are some helpful hints to remember about books:

- When you find a book you really love, see if the author has written other books. You will probably like them too.

- Don't go anywhere without a book. You never know when you'll have some extra time.

- Start a book club with your friends. It's fun to talk about your favorite books. You can trade books, too.

- Books make great gifts—to give or receive. It's fun to start your own library.

- Try to set aside a special time each day for reading.

- If you like to watch TV, see if you can spend as much time reading as you do watching TV.

- Don't ever tell how a book ends. It's not so much fun to read a book when you already know how it ends.

Oh, and by the way...

CONGRATULATIONS!

You've just read a book!

THE END

About the Author

Marilyn Berry has a master's degree in education with a specialization in reading. She is on the staff as a producer and creator of supplementary materials at the Institute of Living Skills. Marilyn is a published author of books and composer of music for children. She is the mother of two sons, John and Brent.